I wish I'd said that!

I wish I'd said that!

An Anthology of Witty Replies
collected by
Kenneth Edwards

Introduced by
Frank Muir

Abelard · London

ISBN 0 200 72467 3 (hardback)
ISBN 0 200 72474 6 (paperback)

Abelard-Schuman Limited
A Member of the Blackie Group
450 Edgware Road
London W2

Printed in Great Britain by
Robert MacLehose & Co. Ltd
Printers to the University of Glasgow

Introduction

by

Frank Muir

Dick Bentley (lab. assistant to mad scientist):
Sir, the bunsen-burner won't work. What shall I do with it?
Jimmy Edwards (mad scientist):
I have an old retort here!

Antique joke from the ancient radio show 'Take it From Here' written by Frank Muir and Denis Norden

Old retorts, as a form of wit, are considerably more ancient than even 'Take It From Here', going back at least as far as Aristotle, who defined wit as 'educated insult'.

The warm glow of satisfaction, the agreeable sense of heightened self-esteem, which accompanies getting off a good riposte has for centuries been one of mankind's favourite forms of ego-inflation. We have, for a splendid second, downed the opposition.

However, there are two problems to be overcome before the splendid moment is ours. The first is to manoeuver our opponent into saying something to which we can make a riposte. The second is to think of a riposte worth making.

In medieval times the first problem was solved by inventing the riddle. In the riddle, as in modern offshoots like 'Knock-Knock', a question is asked which the victim has to ask back; he is thus hooked and ready for the kill. A typical medieval riddle, and one which is still in use, was recorded by a cleric named Bar-Hebraeus who was leader of the Christian community in Syria in the thirteenth century. This went: 'When a cock wakes in the morning, why does he hold one foot in the air?' 'I don't know. When a cock wakes in the morning why *does* he hold one foot in the air?' 'Because if he lifted both he would fall down.' The riddle also had the merit of coming complete with its answer, thus absolving the questioner from any brain work at all.

But riddles, like jokes, are only wit-substitutes. The real stuff, the spontaneous memorable remark, only really came into its own during the Restoration period of the seventeenth century. John Dryden proclaimed that true wit lay in repartee, and the swift rejoinder became socially acceptable at last.

The witty conversational put-down soon became a feature of social life and examples began creeping into biographies. Some of the best of these early examples came from Samuel Johnson. For instance, to the tiresome young man who bemoaned that he had lost all his Greek: 'I believe it happened at the same time, Sir, that I lost all my large estates in Scotland'; to the feeble Sir Thomas Robinson who kept seeing double and asked what he should do about it: 'Count your money!'; to Adam Smith who boasted at considerable length about the beauties of Glasgow: 'Pray, Sir, have you ever seen Brentford?'

Kenneth Edwards has ranged far for this collection. Into his net have gone historical personages, film stars, politicians and playwrights, the famous, the infamous and the unfamous; and perhaps it is the little whiff of envy with which we read the wit of others which makes the book so beguiling. Some of the stories are old friends whose existence we are glad to be reminded of, and some are new friends whose acquaintance we are glad to make, but I think it is true to say that although most of the people who read the book will know some of the anecdotes and a few of the people may know most of them, none of the people will know all of them.

There is a kind of wit which the French call 'l'esprit de l'escalier': the remark that comes to mind too late, as one is already descending the staircase on one's way out. Equally painful is it to hear someone else make the witticism one might have made oneself with a readier presence of mind. Oscar Wilde, overhearing an exceptionally brilliant remark, exclaimed to his friend Whistler, the American painter:

'I wish I'd said that!'

Whistler, knowing Wilde's habit of passing off other people's witticisms as his own, replied with the memorable words:

'You will, Oscar, you will!'

The Ministry of Public Buildings and Works was solemnly considering a new design of lavatory seat for installation in the lavatories of government departments. The official in immediate charge of the matter thought it necessary to consult his superior, and accordingly sent him a memorandum which read:

'I should like to see you on this.'

His superior's reply was:

'At your convenience.'

Groucho Marx was once asked what he thought about sex.

'I think,' he replied, 'that it is here to stay.'

An old lady of 85 was asked at what age a woman ceases to be interested in men.

'Ask me again when I'm a little older' was the reply.

Bernard Shaw, having at one time been cold-shouldered by London society because of his controversial views, subsequently attained such eminence that he was sought after by leading hostesses. One such sent him a card inscribed with the words:

'Lady X will be at home on April 26th.'

The card was promptly returned to her with the following words added:

'So will Bernard Shaw.'

A Hollywood film star returned to Britain to make a film after an absence of ten years. She particularly asked that she should be photographed by the same cameraman as before.

When she saw the rushes, she was disappointed and exclaimed to the cameraman:

'These are not nearly so good as the ones you last took of me.'

'I know, my dear,' replied the cameraman, 'but you must remember that I am ten years older.'

'Tell me, Mrs X, what is your real ground for seeking a divorce from your husband?'

Much-married actress: 'Well, you see, he has turned out to be not at all the kind of husband I am accustomed to.'

In ancient Greece the Spartans—a term applied to all inhabitants of Laconia, the territory of which Sparta was the capital—were noted for their sparing use of words*. It is related that on one occasion the Athenians, their hereditary enemies, sent them a threatening message to the following effect:

'Unless you do as we wish we shall make war on you and, if we defeat you, shall lay waste your country, raze your cities to the ground, slaughter all your men of military age, enslave your women and children, etc.'

To this the Spartans, who were no mean warriors, replied with a two letter word, which in ancient Greek means 'If . . .'

* Hence the English word 'laconic'.

A barrister, having been worsted in a heated dispute with a judge who had flatly contradicted him, finally yielded with the words:

'Yes, my Lord, you are right and I am wrong, as you generally are.'

The Duke of Edinburgh had arrived by air to take part in an important public function and was asked by the leader of the reception committee what the flight had been like.

'Tell me,' enquired the Duke, 'have you ever flown yourself?'

'Oh yes, your Royal Highness,' was the reply, 'often.'

'Well,' said the Duke, 'it was like that.'

During the American Civil War a lady exclaimed effusively to President Lincoln:

'Oh, Mr President, I feel so sure that God is on our side, don't you?'

'Ma'am,' replied the President, 'I am more concerned that we should be on God's side.'

Lord Chesterfield, who lived in the 18th century and is famous for his Letters to his Son, *was conversing with Elizabeth Chudleigh, a lady of doubtful reputation who was widely believed to have given birth to illegitimate twins.*

'Dear Lord Chesterfield,' she said, 'I hope you do not believe the scandalous rumours which are circulating about me.'

'Do not distress yourself, madam,' replied Lord Chesterfield. 'I seldom believe more than half I hear.'

A certain French general named Gaillard, who lived in the time of King Louis XV and was renowned for his gallantry towards women, said, on one occasion, that there was no such thing as an ugly woman. His remark was overheard by a lady whose face was disfigured by a squashed nose and who thereupon accosted him with the words:

'Confess, General, that you are now face to face with a really ugly woman.'

'Not at all, madame,' replied the general, 'You are like all women, an angel fallen from Heaven. You merely had the misfortune to fall on your nose.'

A young composer had written two pieces of music and asked the great Rossini to hear them both and say which he preferred. He duly played one piece, wherupon Rossini intervened.

'You need not play any more,' he said, 'I prefer the other one.'

Winston Churchill and a friend were discussing the merits and demerits of Churchill's political opponent, Clement Atlee, the leader of the Labour Party. In reply to certain criticisms of Attlee, voiced by Churchill, his friend commented:

'Well, you must admit that he's modest.'

'True,' replied Churchill, 'but then he has a lot to be modest about.'

At the close of a hotly disputed lawsuit, counsel for one of the parties became more and more restive as the judge proceeded to sum up against him. He could not openly contradict or criticize the judge, but he went as far as he dared and, whenever the judge said anything with which he disagreed, he sighed, grunted, or fidgeted in his seat. At length the judge could stand it no longer and enquired menacingly:

'Am I to understand, Mr X, that you are seeking to express your contempt of this court?'

'No, my Lord,' replied the barrister, 'I am trying to conceal it.'

'How say you? Are you guilty or not guilty?'
'I can't say till I've heard the evidence.'

An English Evangelical clergyman found himself alone in a French railway compartment with a large Frenchman busily engaged in getting outside the contents of a luncheon basket. Thinking that he should lose no opportunity of spreading the Gospel, especially among people as materialistic as the French, he leaned towards the Frenchman and asked in a low voice:

'Do you love Jesus?'

The Frenchman paused for a moment and then said:

'Yes, I love your English cheeses. But most of all I love our French Camembert.'

The well-known dancer, Isadora Duncan, suggested to Bernard Shaw that they should have a child together.

'Imagine,' she said, 'a child with my body and your brain!'

'Yes,' replied Shaw, 'but suppose it had my body and your brain.'

The late Gilbert Harding fell asleep while attending one of Noel Coward's plays and snored noisily throughout the performance. Afterwards he apologized to Coward, who replied:

'My dear fellow, don't apologize. After all, I have never bored you half as much as you have bored me.'

On the first night of one of his plays Oscar Wilde stood in the foyer of the theatre, receiving bouquets of flowers from his admirers. One member of the audience, who was far from being one of his admirers and wished to humiliate him, presented him with a rotten cabbage.

'Thank you, my dear fellow,' said Wilde, 'Every time I smell it I shall be reminded of you.'

An American lady had warned her negro maid to beware of going out after dark because a rapist was believed to be at large in the neighbourhood.

'Oh my,' replied the maid, 'that sure is terrible. I rape so easy.'

Sir Winston Churchill, on being told that the name of a certain M.P. was 'Bossom', said:
'I see. Neither one thing nor the other.'

During the First World War, a middle-aged man of high standing in the business world, disdaining to pull strings in order to obtain a commission, joined up in the ranks. One day he was afflicted with gastric pains and, having reported sick, was brought before the Medical Officer of his unit, who was, of course, his military superior. (Then, as now, all qualified doctors joining the medical branches of the armed forces were automatically commissioned.)

On his explaining what was wrong, the doctor, a major, was openly contemptuous.

'A stomach ache?' he said, 'Would you come to me with a stomach ache in civil life?'

'No, sir,' replied the patient, standing rigidly to attention, 'I should send for you.'

A celebrated French general, who wished to enjoy the favours of an equally celebrated French courtesan, sent a message which read:
'Ou? Quand? Combien?'
She answered:
'Chez moi. Ce soir. Rien.'

A lady received a card of invitation to a dance at Buckingham Palace and duly attended without having troubled to answer the invitation in writing.

Happening to find herself next to the equerry who had issued the invitations she said:

'I must apologize for not writing to accept your kind invitation. It was very remiss of me.'

'It's quite all right,' replied the equerry 'There's no need to apologize. It's entirely our fault for having invited you.'

Question: 'What do you think of marriage as an institution?'

Reply: 'I think it's fine for people who like living in institutions.'

Mr Stanley Baldwin, when Prime Minister, was sitting in his room at the House of Commons and found himself unable to concentrate because someone with a voice like a foghorn was shouting at the top of his voice in an adjoining room.

'What on earth is that noise?' he asked his Private Secretary.

'I think, sir, that it is Mr X speaking to someone in his constituency.'

'Oh, is it?' rejoined Baldwin. 'Why doesn't he use the telephone?'

Benito Mussolini, the fascist dictator of Italy, had preserved the Italian monarchy but kept all political power in his own hands and reduced the position of the King, Victor Emmanuel, to that of a mere puppet. When Mussolini launched his unprovoked attack on Ethiopia, which was ruled by the Emperor Hailie Selassie, King Emmanuel was asked for his views:

'I really do not care very much whether we win the war or lose it,' he is reported to have said. 'If we win, I shall become Emperor of Ethiopia. If we lose, I may become King of Italy.'

Dr Spooner of Oxford, the originator of 'Spoonerisms', came face to face with a young man who said:

'Good evening, Dr Spooner, I don't suppose you remember me.'

'On the contrary,' replied Spooner. 'I remember your name perfectly, but I've completely forgotten your face.'

A prominent theatrical critic was incensed at not receiving an invitation to the first night of one of Noel Coward's plays. He accordingly sent Coward a note in the following terms:

'Dear Noel,

You did not see fit to send me an invitation to the first night of your new play. Perhaps you will be kind enough to send me an invitation to your second night—if you have a second night.'

Coward replied without delay:

'Dear X,

I am sorry that I omitted to send you an invitation to our first night. I send you herewith two tickets for our second night; one for you and one for a friend—if you have a friend.'

It is related that Bernard Shaw once asked his dining partner whether she would go to bed with a man for five hundred pounds. The lady smirked and said roguishly:

'Well, it would depend on how good looking he was . . .'

'Would you do it for ten bob?' enquired Shaw.

'What do you take me for?' burst out the lady.

'We have already settled that question,' said Shaw drily. 'All we are discussing now is the price.'

It was the opening night of one of Bernard Shaw's plays. After the final curtain there was rapturous applause and, in response to repeated cries of 'Author', Shaw appeared on stage. The applause was redoubled, but one loud-voiced member of the audience expressed his disapproval of the play by shouting at the top of his voice:

'Rotten!' 'Nonsense!' 'Rubbish!' Despite the general hubbub, Shaw heard him and shouted back:

'I agree with you, my friend. But what are we against so many?'

It is related that Cyrus the Great, founder of the Persian Empire in the 6th century B.C., *had occasion to reprove his son Cambyses for arrogant behaviour. He added, as many a father has done before and since:*

'When I was your age I never spoke to my father as you speak to me.'

'No,' replied Cambyses, 'but you were the son of a comparative nobody, whereas I am the son of Cyrus the Great.'

Mark Twain, the well-known American writer, discovered that reports of his death were circulating. Asked for his comments he replied:

'The reports of my death have been much exaggerated.'

Country vicar to aged villager:
'How is it that I haven't seen you at church lately?'
Aged villager, after profound thought:
'I ain't been.'

Schoolboy to form master:

'Please, sir, can I be punished for something I haven't done?'

'Of course not.'

'Thank you, sir, I'm afraid I haven't done my homework, sir.'

A press reporter once asked the great Italian composer Giuseppe Verdi for his full address.

'I think,' replied Verdi, 'that Italy will be sufficient.'

Question: 'Is life worth living?'

Reply: 'It depends on the liver.'

(Attributed to Sir Herbert Tree).

Kruschev, when he was still master of Russia, was discoursing before a large audience on the iniquities perpetrated by Stalin, when a voice at the back of the hall cried out:

'You were one of his colleagues, why didn't you stop him?'

In the terrible silence which followed not a man in the audience moved a muscle. Raking the assembly with his eyes, Kruschev thundered:

'Who said that?'

But still not a man moved and the tension was becoming unbearable when Kruschev said quietly:

'Now you know why.'

In the course of a lawsuit the famous American artist Whistler was asked, in relation to a picture which he had taken only two days to paint, whether it was true that he asked two hundred guineas for only two days' work.

'Oh, no,' was the reply. 'I ask that for the knowledge of a lifetime.'

In communist Hungary an agricultural inspector from Budapest, the capital, was questioning a local farmer about that year's potato crop.

'Comrade Inspector,' declared the latter, 'under the beneficent rule of Communism the potatoes produced by the collective farms are so numerous that, if they were piled together in a single heap, they would reach as far as the feet of God Almighty.'

'Don't be absurd, Comrade,' snapped the inspector, 'you know very well that God is imaginary.'

'True, Comrade Inspector,' was the reply, 'but so are the potatoes.'

A timid looking little man in a restaurant accosted a stranger who was on the point of leaving:

'Excuse me,' he said, 'but are you Mr John Smith of Newcastle?'

'No,' replied the stranger, mystified.

'Well,' said the little man, 'I am. And that is his overcoat you've just put on.'

The aging but still active French comedian, Maurice Chevalier, was asked how he felt about old age.
'I prefer it,' he said, 'to the alternative.'

F. E. Smith, the brilliant barrister who was later to become the first Earl of Birkenhead and to hold many high offices, including that of Lord Chancellor, was conducting an extremely complicated case before a rather slow-witted judge. Towards the end of the proceedings the judge intimated that he found the complexity of the case too much for him, whereupon Smith proceeded, with the consent of the other side, to give, in an amazingly short space of time, a masterly summary of the evidence and the points at issue. But the judge seemed as much in the dark as ever and remarked querulously:

'I am sorry, Mr Smith, but I am none the wiser.'
Smith paused, sighed deeply, and replied:
'No, my Lord. But you are better informed.'

At an ambassadorial banquet, after everyone was seated, one of the lady guests complained a little too loudly that, according to the official order of precedence, she ought to be seated next to the ambassador. She was found to be right and several of the guests had to get up and move down in order to make room for her next to her host.

Feeling somewhat conscience-stricken at the fuss she had made, the lady said to the ambassador:
'*You and your wife must find these questions of precedence extremely troublesome.*'
'*Not really,*' *was the reply,* '*we have found by experience that the people who matter don't mind and the people who mind don't matter.*'

Edward Carson, the famous Irish advocate, was cross-examining a hostile witness.

'You drink, don't you?' he enquired.

'That's my business,' rejoined the witness.

'Have you any other business?' asked Carson and promptly sat down.

Notorious bore to Oscar Wilde:
'*I passed your house yesterday.*'
Wilde:
'*Thank you so much.*'

An Irish Protestant who was dangerously ill and believed he was dying sent for a Catholic priest and was received into the Roman Church. His Protestant friends were horrified and one of them asked him how he could thus forsake the creed for which he had stood all his life and go over to the enemy.

'Well,' said the sick man, 'it's this way. I said to myself, if anyone's got to die, better one of their lot than one of our lot.'

Young exquisite encountering a lady in the street:
'I'm terribly sorry I forgot your party yesterday evening, Mrs X.'
Mrs X:
'Oh, weren't you there?'

Lady to the Duke of Wellington:
'What a glorious thing must be a victory, sir!'
'The greatest tragedy in the world, madam, except a defeat.'

Disraeli, who was about to stand for election to Parliament as Member for Marylebone, was asked:
'On what do you propose to stand?'
'On my head,' was the reply.

St Patrick's Day is celebrated with especial fervour in America by those of Irish descent, and Irish green is much in evidence. A lady driving through New York on St Patrick's Day inadvertently crashed the red lights and was alarmed to see a burly policeman bearing down on her with a menacing scowl on his craggy face.

'An' what might ye be doin' droivin past the red loight?' demanded the policeman. 'Is it colour-bloind ye are?'

Recognizing from his brogue that, like many members of the New York police force, the man was Irish, the lady was visited by an inspiration.

'Why, officer,' she said, 'everything looks green to me today.'

'Droive on, ma'am,' said the policeman, his face creased in a delighted smile.

The American artist, Whistler, had been commissioned to paint the portrait of an exceptionally ugly man and the two of them were contemplating the finished work.

'Well,' exclaimed the subject of the portrait, 'you can't call that a great work of art.'

'Perhaps not,' replied Whistler, 'but then you can hardly call yourself a great work of Nature.'

A questionnaire circulated by a Russian government department for the purpose of establishing prospective population trends contained the following questions:

(1) Where were you born?
(2) Where did you go to school?
(3) Where did you attain your majority?
(4) Where would you wish to live?

The answers given by one of the recipients were:

(1) St Petersburg
(2) Petrograd
(3) Leningrad
(4) St Petersburg

The household of a Victorian bishop had been augmented by the addition of a boy, one of whose duties it was to wake his master in the morning and bring him his shaving water. He was told that he must knock on the door of the Bishop's bedroom and, when the bishop asked who was there, to reply:

'The boy, my Lord.'

When the time came, the boy knocked nervously on the door of the bishop's bedroom and, on receiving the expected reply 'Who is there?', was so paralysed by fright that he replied:

'The Lord, my boy.'

An ambitious young executive in a large company, who wanted at all costs to get on, came home some hours earlier than usual and, through his half-open bedroom door, saw his wife in bed with his managing director. Pale and shaken he left the house and encountered one of his colleagues to whom he related what had happened. The colleague was sympathetic and condoled with him on his wife's infidelity.

'But you don't understand,' was the reply. 'He nearly saw me.'

X, a leader of the Canadian Conservative Party in the last century was a heavy drinker. One day he appeared on the same platform as his principal political opponent. While the latter was making his speech, X, who was completely drunk, was violently sick in full view of the spectators.

His opponent, feeling that his victory was now assured, cut short his speech and sat down. But X was not yet beaten, and after a moment's pause staggered to his feet and said:

'I apologize, ladies and gentlemen, but whenever I hear that man speak, I can't help being sick.'

Beau Brummel, who was the undisputed leader of fashion in the days of the Regency, was once told that a certain gentleman was so well dressed that everyone turned to look at him.

'In that case,' replied Brummel, 'he was not well dressed.'

Louis XIV of France was an autocrat and required from all his subjects not only absolute obedience but, as the following anecdote shows, something more.

The King had commanded that the Count de X, one of his ministers, should wait upon him at 11 a.m. At five minutes to eleven he observed from the window of his room in Versailles the arrival of the mimister's coach in the courtyard of the palace.

Fully expecting that his visitor would be at least one minute late for his appointment, Louis fumed inwardly and his anger was not appeased by the fact that, just as the palace clock was striking eleven, the doors of his room were thrown open to admit the minister, who advanced into the room, bowed low, and said:

'A votre service, Majesté.'

'Monsieur,' replied the King indignantly, 'je vous ai presqu' attendu.'

It was noticed that a certain actress who was well on the way to stardom went out of her way to be kind and considerate to the humblest members of the film and theatrical world. When someone praised her for this, she replied:

'It's always wise to make friends on the way up. One may need them on the way down.'

Diogenes, who flourished about 380 B.C., founded the school of philosophy whose followers, known as the Cynics, affected to despise all worldly possessions and all man-made laws and conventions. Diogenes himself is reputed to have lived in a barrel and it is related that one day, while sunning himself in his barrel, he was visited by no less a person than Alexander the Great, who, standing between him and the sun's rays, enquired whether there was anything he wanted.

'Yes,' replied the sage, 'I should like you to stand out of my light.'

A little girl, fresh from a school sex-talk, said to her mother:

'Mummy, do you and Daddy have sexual relations?

'Yes, dear,' replied her mother. 'Why do you ask?'

'Well,' replied the little girl, 'why haven't I met any of them?'

'Well, Celia dear, did you enjoy Mrs X's children's party? And did you thank her for having you and giving you a nice time?'

'Yes, mother, but I shortened it a bit. I said: "Thank you, Mrs X, I've been very nicely had." '

Towards the end of the last world war, British forces under General Montgomery (as he then was) and American forces under General Patton were operating close together. Unfortunately there was bad blood between the two commanders and, in the course of some dispute between them, Montgomery sent Patton the following message:

'I have only two things to say to you. First, keep out of my way. Secondly, leave me your petrol.'

Very soon after this, Patton's forces achieved a spectacular advance, far outdistancing the British forces, and Patton sent a young American officer to Montgomery with a single can of petrol and the following reply, which was delivered orally.

'General Patton thanks you for your communication. He hopes you feel that he and his forces are now sufficiently far out of your way; and he sends you this can of petrol, which is all he can spare.'

A youth had to fill in a questionnaire which contained a number of headings including 'Name', 'Nationality', 'Age', 'Sex', 'Place of Birth' and 'Religion'. He had no difficulty in supplying most of the information asked for, but was a little puzzled by the heading 'Sex'.
After some thought he wrote 'Occasionally'.

A nervous young curate was visiting one of his parishioners, a sharp-tongued old lady, in the late autumn.
'Well,' he said, 'winter draws on, eh?'
'As a matter of fact I have,' replied the old lady tartly, 'though I can't see what business it is of yours.'

An American journalist was determined to find out for himself how the Polish people felt about Stalin, who was then still alive and in power. He accordingly obtained permission from the Polish authorities to visit Warsaw and, on his arrival there, was introduced to an English-speaking Pole who was to act as his official guide.

Having been shown round Warsaw, the American invited his guide to dine with him in a restaurant and, at the end of the meal, asked the question he had been meaning to ask from the beginning:

'How do you feel about Stalin?'

At these words the Pole blanched and in a low voice said:

'Come outside.'

Both of them accordingly left the restaurant and, once outside, the American repeated his question. But the Pole merely shook his head and explained that it would be necessary to make a journey by tram. They accordingly boarded one and did not leave it until it had reached its terminus in a remote suburb of the city.

The American, now quite out of patience, demanded an immediate answer to his question. The Pole, after peering anxiously over each shoulder (notwithstanding that the street was completely deserted), brought his lips close to one of the American's ears and whispered hoarsely:

'You asked me how I feel about Stalin. Well, I rather like him.'

A benevolent but forgetful old gentleman was entertaining a party of people, some of whom he had not met for a long time. As they were all standing around drinking cocktails before going in to dinner, the host moved from one to the other making polite conversation. In the course of so doing he came upon a young man of whom he had not heard for some time.

'I am delighted to see you,' he beamed. 'And how is my dear old friend, your father?'

'I am sorry to have to tell you, sir,' said the young man, 'that my father died some six months ago.'

The host expressed his deep regret and at that moment the butler announced that dinner was served.

After dinner, the host again espied the young man and, having completely forgotten the previous conversation, enquired once more after his dear old friend, the young man's father.

'I am sorry, sir,' was the reply, 'but my father is *still* dead.'

'What do you think of publishing as a career?'
'Well, it's better than working.'

An Irish priest, revisiting his old parish in the spring, observed a very old man, who had been a member of his congregation, approaching.

'Why, Pat,' he called delightedly, 'so you are still with us, I am glad to see. How ever do you manage it?'

'Well, Your Reverence,' replied the old man, "tis this way. I find that if I don't doy in winter I don't doy any other toime of the year.'

A man who had just bought a pint of beer in a public house remembered that he had a telephone call to make and, in order to deter anyone from drinking his beer in his absence, wrote—untruthfully—on a piece of paper which he left beside his tankard the words:

'I have spat in this beer.'

On his return he found the beer intact, but someone had written on the piece of paper the words:

'So have I.'

Towards the end of his life, Sir Winston Churchill was interviewed by a young reporter who expressed his thanks and added:

'Perhaps I may have the privilege of meeting you again—er—next year?'

'I don't see why not,' replied Churchill. 'You look a healthy young man, and ought to survive until then.'

The great Swiss zoologist and geologist, Agassiz, a Professor at the University of Cambridge, Massachusetts, was invited to lecture in New York, but declined on the ground that he was too busy. He was then offered an enormous sum to lecture but, to the astonishment of the New Yorkers, again declined with the words:

'I simply have no time to earn money.'

Victorian bishop to page-boy:
'Who is it, my boy, before whom we all tremble and before whom even I am as a worm?'
Page-boy, with bated breath:
'The missus, Sir.'

Englishman, offering his cigarette-case to a Frenchman:
'*Etes-vous un fumier,* Monsieur?*'
Frenchman, after a barely perceptible pause:
'*Oui, Monsieur.*'

* *a dung-heap*

A distinguished barrister, notorious for his sharp tongue and the subtle way in which he often expressed his lack of respect for some of the judges before whom he appeared, was conducting a case before three judges in the Court of Appeal.

At the end of the first day's hearing, the President of the Court announced that one of the three judges would be unable to attend on the following day, and asked the barrister whether he had any objection to continuing the case before only two judges.

'That depends, my Lord,' replied the barrister, 'which two?'

During the First World War, well-off people with large houses in London or elsewhere converted them into minor hospitals or convalescent homes and, if suitably qualified, themselves served as members of the nursing staff.

A young lady interested in a wounded officer who was being cared for in one of these establishments approached the matron and asked whether she could see Lieutenant X.

'We do not allow ordinary visitors,' said the matron. 'May I ask whether you are a relation?'

'Oh, yes,' said the young lady boldly. 'I'm his sister.'

'Really,' was the reply, 'I am very glad to meet you. I'm his mother.'

An elderly, very prim and proper school-mistress found herself in a spot affording a comprehensive view of the Tower of London. Not without embarrassment, she accosted a passing policeman and said:

'Excuse me, officer, which is the—er—Bloody Tower?'

The policeman smiled indulgently and, indicating with a wave of his arm the whole of the Tower buildings, replied:

'All of it, Mum, all of it.'

Psychiatrist to patient:
'Are you ever troubled by immoral thoughts?'
Patient:
'No, Doctor. I rather enjoy them.'

A man accused of a criminal offence elected to give evidence in his own defence. When he had taken the oath, the judge reminded him that he was now bound to tell the truth and that, if he failed to do so, he would be committing perjury, which was a very serious offence.

'That's all very well, my Lord,' said the accused man, 'but the last time I told the truth in court I got six months.'

A former mistress wrote to the Duke of Wellington and threatened to make certain love letters he had written to her public unless he made it worth her while not to. His reply was:
'Dear Jenny,
    Publish and be damned,
        Yours affectionately,
            Wellington.'

Sam Goldwyn, when told that his son was engaged to be married, is reported to have replied:

'Thank Heaven. A bachelor's life is no life for a single man.'

A lady related to the noble family of which the Earl of Carlisle was the head was somewhat autocratic in her dealings with the inhabitants of the local village and, when her husband was standing for Parliament, decided that the local villagers must vote for him.

She accordingly summoned them all to a meeting in the Parish Hall where she expounded the policy of her husband's party and as good as ordered all present to vote for him.

At the end of her address there was, at first, a dead silence. Then one of the villagers rose awkwardly to his feet and said:

'Thank you, ma'am, thank you kindly. That's what you thinks. We thinks otherwise.'

An opponent of the Labour Party was invited by a pro-Labour friend to agree that the Labour Government, then in office, had done well.

'They have certainly achieved more than I expected,' was the reply. 'But then I didn't expect them to achieve much.'

Dean Inge, the Dean of St Paul's Cathedral, was also a journalist. On arrival in America he was asked whether it was true to say that he was a pillar of the Anglican Church.

'I don't know about that,' he replied, 'but I am two columns in the Evening Standard.'

Conversation between two old Cockney women:
'You don't 'arf look awful, you don't.'
'Who do?'
'You don't.'

A battalion-commander, accompanied by his sergeant-major, came upon one of his men lying on his face and radiating a powerful smell of whisky.
'This man's dead drunk, sergeant-major,' he said. 'You'll have to put him on a charge.'
'Begging your pardon, sir,' said the sergeant-major, wishing to do his best for the man, 'he ain't drunk. I seen 'im move.'

An infatuated young man was sending his girl-friend a telegram which read:
'Ozzy loves his Woozy Woozy Woozy.'
'You can have another "Woozy" without it costing any more,' said the post office clerk.
'No, thanks,' replied the young man after a pause for reflection, 'I think that would sound rather silly.

It was proposed that, for political reasons, a young German prince should marry a Spanish princess whom he had never met. Not unnaturally, the prince declined to commit himself without knowing what his proposed bride looked like, and a picture of her, executed by her father's court painter, was accordingly sent to him.

The young man examined the picture critically.

'This is a very bad likeness,' he said. 'The eyes are too bright; the hair too luxuriant; the features too regular; the figure too shapely.'

'But,' he was asked, 'does your Highness know the young lady?'

'No,' replied the young man, 'but I know court painters.'

When the Earl of Home (later Sir Alec Douglas Home) became Conservative Prime Minister in succession to Mr Macmillan, Mr Wilson, the leader of the Labour Opposition, criticized the appointment as Prime Minister in a democratic country of a fourteenth earl. In reply to this criticism, Lord Home said that, when one came to think of it, Mr Wilson could be the fourteenth Mr Wilson.

A man was warned by his doctor against too much high living.

'Can you guarantee, doctor,' he asked, 'that if I give up drinking, smoking and sex I shall live longer?'

'No,' replied the doctor, 'but it will seem longer.'

Lord Curzon, who was at one time British Foreign Secretary, was making a tour of Japan by car, accompanied by a Japanese guide-interpreter. At one point in their journey, they came across a number of women, old and young, bathing naked in a wayside pond. Curzon stopped the car and gazed for a full minute at the shocking sight. Then he turned to the guide and asked whether it was not considered improper in Japan for people to bathe naked in a public place.

'No,' was the embarrassed reply. 'But it is considered improper to watch people bathing naked in a public place.'

A critic of the first post-war Labour administration was invited by one of its supporters to concede that a recent action by the Prime Minister, Mr Attlee (as he then was) reflected great credit on him.

'Yes,' said the other, 'I confess that my opinion of him has risen almost to zero.'

J. H. Thomas, the Labour minister, once said to Lord Birkenhead:

'Oh, Birkenhead, I've got a 'orrible 'eadache. What do you suggest?'

'What about a couple of aspirates?' replied Birkenhead.

The well-known journalist and politician Horatio Bottomley had called on a certain Lord Cholmondeley (pronounced Chumley) and, when the butler opened the door in answer to his ring, enquired whether Lord Cholmondeley was at home. He pronounced the name exactly as it is spelt and the butler, seeking to correct him, replied that Lord 'Chumley' was at home.

'Good,' replied Bottomley. 'Tell him that Horatio Bumley would like a word with him.'

Talleyrand, the famous French statesman, who was slightly lame, had occasion to pay his respects to an influential lady of the court who suffered from a slight squint. He duly limped across the room to make his bow and, as he did so, the lady enquired:

'Comment vous portez-vous, Monsieur Talleyrand?'

This is, of course, normal French for 'How are you?' but translated literally means 'How do you carry yourself?' The way in which the lady spoke the words and smiled at her ladies behind her fan made it clear that she was taunting Talleyrand (who was no favourite of hers) with his lameness. Without hesitation Talleyrand replied:

'Comme vous voyez, madame,' which could either mean 'As you see, madame'—a perfectly polite rejoinder—or 'I walk as crookedly as you look'.

To a lady who said that a certain landscape reminded her of his painting, James Whistler was said to have replied:
'Yes, madam, Nature is creeping up.'

Billy Hughes, the Australian politician, wore a glass eye so exactly like his real eye that many people could not tell the difference.

In the course of some tough bargaining which threatened to end in deadlock, Hughes said that he would yield on one condition, namely, that his opponent should tell him which of his eyes was the glass one.

'The left,' said the other without hesitation.

'Quite right,' said Hughes. 'How do you know?'

'Because it's so much kinder than the other,' was the reply.

The late Queen of Tonga, who took part in the coronation procession of Elizabeth II, won all hearts by keeping the hood of her carriage down despite the rain and by smiling and waving to spectators all along the route.

The Queen was an ample lady, not unlike most people's idea of a cannibal queen, and opposite her in the carriage sat a little man about half her size.

'Who's that?' somebody asked Noel Coward.

'Probably her lunch,' he replied.

Robert Browning, the poet, was asked by his future wife, Elizabeth Moulton-Barrett, what an exceptionally obscure passage in one of his poems meant. Having puzzled over the passage for some time, Browning gave up the struggle.

'Miss Barret,' he said, 'when that passage was written only God and Robert Browning knew what it meant. Now only God knows.'

Denis Compton, the well-known cricketer, was constantly being asked for his autograph.

'Don't you mind the way people keep pestering you?' asked a friend.

'Yes,' replied Compton, 'but I shall mind it a lot more when they stop.'

During the First World War, anti-German feeling was so strong that people with German-sounding names made haste to change them by deed poll, and people of known German descent were regarded with the greatest suspicion.

A young officer in the British Army was known to have German connections, and his CO considered it necessary to take the matter up with him.

'Tell me, Captain X,' he said, 'exactly how German are you?'

'Just as much as the King, sir,' was the reply. (King George V had a German grandfather, Prince Albert, and a half-German grandmother, Queen Victoria.)

Calvin Coolidge, the President of the United States, was known for his taciturnity. On one occasion he had been to church alone and, on his return, his wife questioned him about the sermon. What had it been about?

'Sin,' replied Coolidge laconically.

'Well, what had the preacher to say about sin?' demanded Mrs Coolidge.

Her husband remained for some moments plunged in thought and then replied:

'He's against it.'

A timid female witness was being mercilessly heckled by cross-examining counsel and was reduced to such a state that she could not answer his fusillade of questions.

'Why don't you answer?' asked the judge gently.

'Oh, my Lord, he frightens me so,' said the witness.

'So he does me, Madam,' replied the judge grimly.

The man who was later to become Pope John XXIII was serving as Papal Nuncio in Paris and, when his term of office was about to expire, was much disturbed by the thought that his next appointment might be to a post in the Vatican.

On being asked why, he is said to have replied:

'It's no fun working so near the boss.'

A young lady at a French banquet asked her French dining partner why he had been appointed an officer of the Legion of Honour.

'Well,' he replied, 'for one thing, I never asked indiscreet questions.'

A very recently qualified young doctor was receiving his first patient, a man who complained of a rash on his chest, and asked what was wrong with him.

'Have you ever had this before?' enquired the doctor, mystified.

'Yes,' replied the patient, 'about two years ago.'

'Oh,' replied the doctor after a pause, 'well—er— you've got it again.'

A young man was telling a middle-aged, worldly-wise widow about his quarrel with his girl friend.

'Well,' she remarked, 'there is nothing for it. You will have to admit you were in the wrong and apologize.'

'But,' exclaimed the young man, 'haven't you been listening? I was in the right and *she* was in the wrong.'

'If that is really so,' replied the widow, 'you will have to take some flowers as well.'

President Calvin Coolidge found himself sitting next to a young lady at a public dinner. Bringing all her charm to bear, the young lady said archly:

'Mr President, I have made a bet with my friends that I can make you say at least three words to me during dinner.'

'You lose,' replied Coolidge grimly and relapsed into his customary silence for the rest of the meal.

Marilyn Monroe, before she became a great film star, earned money by posing in the nude. After she had attained stardom a reporter asked her:

'Did you really have nothing on when you posed for those pictures?'

'Oh, no,' smiled Marilyn, 'I had the radio on.'

The famous cartoonist, Giles, was reproved in a letter from his editor for unpunctuality and unreliability—faults to which the editor himself was notoriously prone.

Giles' reply was as follows:

'Dear Pot,

Thank you for your letter,

        Kettle.'

A young man sitting next to a very attractive woman at dinner found himself at a loss for conversation and said, merely for the sake of saying something:

'I hate that man sitting opposite to us.'

'You mean the man with the moustache?' asked the young woman. 'That's my brother.'

'No, no,' stammered the young man hastily, 'I mean the one without the moustache.'

'That's my husband,' said the young woman.

'I know,' replied the young man with remarkable presence of mind, 'that's why I hate him.'

During the Second World War a young army officer was stopped in Whitehall by a stranger to London, who asked him which side the War Office was on.

'Well,' replied the young officer ruefully, 'they're supposed to be on our side.'

'I say, waiter, I've tasted fresher fish than this!'

'Maybe, Sir, but not 'ere.'

A Jewish shopkeeper who believed he was dying perceived very dimly—for his eyesight was failing—some figures standing beside his bed.

'*Is my wife Miriam here?*' *he asked.*

'*Yes, dear, I am here.*'

'*And my son Jacob?*'

'*Yes, father, I am here,*'

'*And my daughter, Rebecca?*'

'*Yes, father.*'

Upon this the supposedly dying man sat bolt upright in bed and said in a voice of thunder:

'*THEN WHO IS LOOKING AFTER THE SHOP?*'

A French general was once asked by a journalist whether there was any truth in the story that a certain battle which he was reputed to have won had really been won by his second in command.

'I don't know,' replied the general, 'but I do know this. If the battle had been lost, I should have lost it.'

Dorothy Parker, the American authoress, was discussing with another woman a man whom they both knew.

'*You must admit,*' *said the friend,* '*that he is always courteous to his inferiors.*'

'*Where does he find them?*' *asked Miss Parker.*

A former head of Queen's College, Oxford, had a reputation for omniscience. It seemed impossible to raise any subject with which he was not familiar. Accordingly, two of his fellow dons at Queen's read up the most abstruse subject they could find in the encyclopaedia, and discoursed learnedly upon it at their next meeting with him.

He listened to them for a little time and then, when invited to comment, replied drily:

'Since writing that article in the encyclopaedia I have changed my views.'

Club bore, having recounted a hoary anecdote:
'And the extraordinary thing is that it happened to my father.'

Victim: 'What is even more extraordinary is that I seem to have met at least twenty of your brothers.'

At an ecclesiastical gathering a very earnest young clergyman who spent much of his time trying to Christianize factory workers was asked about his work by one of his superiors.

'I'm taking God into Industry,' said the young man.

'How interesting for Him,' replied the other. 'Where are you planning to take Him next?'

In the days when the University authorities exercised a much stricter control over the non-academic activities of the students than they do now, a young student at Oxford was discovered by the Proctor* arm in arm with a lady of the streets. The following conversation ensued:

Proctor: 'Your name and college, please.'

Student: 'X of St Y's College.'

Proctor: 'And who, may I ask, is this lady?'

Student: 'She's my sister.'

Proctor (with asperity): 'Don't be absurd, sir. She's a known prostitute.'

Student: 'I know. Mother's terribly cut up about it.'

* *One of the University dons responsible for discipline.*

A young man championing the works of an ultramodern writer and seeking to convince a friend of their excellence, said that they would be read when Homer and Shakespeare were forgotten.

'And not until,' replied his friend.

Whistler and a friend were discussing the Boer War, which was then going against the British, and the friend was extolling the merits of the general commanding the British forces, Sir Redvers Buller, who, he said, had withdrawn from a certain engagement 'without losing a man, a gun, or a flag.'

'Or a minute,' added Whistler.

A lady buying some fruit at a greengrocer's explained that she wanted it for her husband, who was ill, and asked whether it had been sprayed with poisonous fertilizer or anything like that.

'No, madam,' replied the greengrocer. 'You'll have to get that from the chemist.'

A conscientious young schoolmistress made a point of getting to know the parents of all her pupils. One day she was travelling by bus and saw, sitting opposite to her, a man who, she felt sure, was one of the parents whose acquaintance she had made. She accordingly smiled brightly at him and was seriously disconcerted when he not only did not smile back, but said coldly:

'I don't think I know you, madam.'

Thoroughly flustered, the young woman, realizing she must have made a mistake, blurted out:

'I'm terribly sorry. I thought you were the father of one of my children.'

The Duke of Wellington was once accosted by a stranger who exclaimed:

'Mr Jones, I believe.'

'Sir,' replied the Duke, 'if you believe that you will believe anything.'

When General de Gaulle was in Algiers during the war, he called a hurried meeting of the Free French National Committee. One of his ministers arrived in shorts, pullover and gym shoes, having received the summons while he was on the beach. De Gaulle looked at him coldly and said:
   'Haven't you forgotten something?'
   'What?' asked the minister.
   'Your hoop,' replied de Gaulle.

Labouchère, the journalist and politician, was conversing with a friend in the lounge of a London club and was commenting very outspokenly on various contemporary notabilities. Their talk was was taking place within easy earshot of an elderly gentleman, who became progressively more indignant and eventually accosted Labouchère with the words:
   'Young man, I knew your grandmother!'
   'Have I by any chance the honour of addressing my grandfather?' replied Labouchère.

Dorothy Parker and a glamorous film actress were both about to pass through the same doorway when the actress drew back with the words 'Age before beauty.'
   'Yes, my dear,' replied Miss Parker, 'and pearls before swine.'

Margot (pronounced Margo) Asquith, wife of Henry Asquith, who was British Prime Minister at the outbreak of the First World War and later received an earldom, was attending a party in Hollywood at which Jean Harlow was present. The latter approached her and said:

'Why, you are Margott Asquith, aren't you?'

'No, my dear,' replied the peeress. 'The 't' is silent as in Harlow.'

The Victorian statesman Lord Palmerston, who was strongly disapproved of by Queen Victoria and her consort, but was popular among the common people by reason of his eccentricities, his amours and his general zest for life, was suffering from what was proved to be his last illness. His doctor tactfully suggested to him that he might be well advised to put his house in order just in case he should die.

'Die, my dear doctor!' replied Palmerston with unconscious humour, 'That's the last thing I shall do.'

A country parson was congratulating one of his flock on the success with which he had transformed a plot of waste land into a beautiful garden.

'It is indeed wonderful,' he said, 'what man can achieve with the help of Almighty God.'

'Yes, sir,' was the reply, 'but you should have seen the place when only the Almighty was looking after it.'

When Herbert Asquith, after his retirement from the Premiership, was created Earl of Oxford and Asquith, Lloyd George, the leader of the Liberal Party, was asked for his comments. He replied:
'I envy him neither his Ox nor his Ass.'

Dorothy Parker, the famous American authoress and wit, received while she was abroad a cable from a friend of hers announcing the birth of a baby. She immediately cabled back:
'Many congratulations. We knew you had it in you.'

A man convicted of a criminal offence was asked whether he had anything to say before sentence was passed.
'Yes,' he shouted, 'as God is my judge I am innocent.'
'You're mistaken,' replied the judge. 'He isn't; I am; you aren't; six months.'

'Was the butcher rude to you again when you telephoned him this morning, Mary?'
'Yes, M'lady, he was. But I soon put 'im in his place. "'Oo the bloody 'ell do you think you're talkin' to," I says. "This ain't the cook speaking, this is 'er Ladyship." '

An elderly private was brought to the orderly room on a charge of having a dirty rifle.

'Ah,' said the presiding officer, 'a very old soldier. What were you charged with the last time you appeared in the orderly room?'

Stung to sarcasm, the man replied:

"Avin a dirty bow and 'arrer, sir.'

A conceited young clergyman delivered a sermon and sought his bishop's opinion of it.

'Well,' said the bishop, 'since you ask me, I think your sermon resembled the great sword of Charlemagne.'

'It was a victorious sword, was it not?' replied the young man, deeply flattered.

'Yes,' said the bishop, 'it was. But it was also long and flat.'

In the smoking room of a London club several men were engaged in a heated argument in the course of which Mr Smith was unnecessarily offensive to Mr Brown, who rose abruptly and made for the door.

'Goodnight,' one of the men called after him.

'Goodnight, gentlemen,' was the reply, 'goodnight, Mr Smith.'

The party wall separating Heaven from Hell had developed cracks through which sulphurous fumes emanating from the latter place penetrated into the former, much to the discomfort of its inhabitants. The Lord accordingly called upon Old Nick to abate the nuisance without delay, but was told by the latter that he had taken legal advice and had been assured that he was under no liability. No reply was received from the Lord for some little time. When it came it was in the following terms:

'Dear Nick,

You win. Have been unable to obtain any legal advice whatever.'

Woman to elderly coloured man who had just offered her his seat in a crowded bus:
'*I don't like to deprive you.*'
The coloured man waved her objections aside:
'*No depravity ma'am,*' *he assured her.*

A British minesweeper was moored alongside a gigantic American aircraft carrier. A seaman in the American vessel called out to one in the British:

'Well, bud, how's the world's second biggest navy?'

'O.K.,' came the reply, 'how's its second best?'

A lecturer at a theological college informed his class that the subject of his next lecture would be the sin of deceit and that, by way of preparation, he wished them all to read the 17th chapter of St Mark's Gospel. When the time came he asked how many members of his class had complied with his instructions. Every one of them raised his right hand.

'Thank you,' said the lecturer. 'It is to people like you that today's lecture is especially addressed. There is no 17th Chapter of Mark.'

The late Pope John XXIII, when asked how many people worked in the Vatican, replied with a smile:

'About half of them.'

It is related that John Knox, the famous Scottish divine, who fulminated from the pulpit against Mary Queen of Scots, imposed the strictest discipline on members of his family. On one occasion, when his daughter was late for breakfast, he greeted her with the words:

'Child of the Devil.'

Her reply was:

'Good morning, father.'

The much-esteemed French actor Régnier was acting in a play which required him, at one point, to turn to the right and greet another actor approaching from that direction with the words 'So there you are!' On the first night Régnier, at the appropriate point in the play, turned right and uttered the words 'Ah, so there you are!' before he realized that his fellow actor, for some inexplicable reason, was approaching him from the left. Quick as a flash Régnier swung round and added the words 'I saw you in the mirror.'

A gentleman on being presented to the Duke of Wellington said:
'This is the proudest moment of my life.'
The Duke:
'Don't be a fool, sir!'

Somerset Maugham, asked why he preferred to sail in non-British ships, replied:
'Because, in non-British ships, there's none of that nonsense about women and children first.'

A man bearing the distinguished name of Cave-Brown-Cave had occasion to telephone a man whose name was Home. 'Hullo,' he said, 'this is Cave-Brown-Cave speaking.'
'Really?' was the reply. 'This is Home-Sweet-Home.'

At a political meeting the candidate concluded his address by asking whether anybody had any questions to ask.

'Yes,' said a member of the audience. 'Why is the Union Jack at the back of the hall upside down?'

'I can only assume,' said the candidate, 'that those responsible for decorating the hall were so unfamiliar with our glorious flag as not to know how it should be hung.'

'Well,' rejoined the questioner, 'it isn't upside down.'

A relative of the compiler, Sir Hubert Murray, a brother of Professor Gilbert Murray O.M., was Lieutenant-Governor of Papua, an Australian dependency. Though the mildest of men, he cordially disliked another public servant who was on the point of retirement and, after taking legal advice, issued the following in a local paper:

'We have all learned, with great regret, of the impending retirement of Sir A B. It is understood that his destined successor, Sir X Y, is a scholar and a gentleman.'

Voltaire, on being asked what he thought of a certain poem entitled 'To Posterity', replied:

'I am afraid it will never reach its address.'

King George I of England was travelling by coach on the continent and stopped at a country inn, where he was charged a preposterous price for a meal consisting of three eggs.

'Are eggs so scarce in this part of the country?' he demanded.

'No, Your Majesty,' replied the innkeeper, 'but kings are.'

During the 'troubles' in Ireland before the establishment of the Irish Free State (now Eire) in 1922 two Irish gunmen with loaded rifles were lying in wait for an unpopular landlord.

'He's very late,' said one of them.

'Yes,' said the other, 'I hope the poor gentleman hasn't met with an accident.'

President Calvin Coolidge was, as related elsewhere, a man of few words. He also slept a good deal, by day as well as by night, and was the reverse of animated.

When he died after completing his term of office, Dorothy Parker, on being told that he was dead, asked:

'How can they tell?'

Air Chief Marshal Sir Robert Brooke-Popham was visiting a friend and, since he was on his way to a Royal Levée, was wearing full dress uniform with medals and decorations. The front door was opened to him by a nervous little maidservant, to whom the visitor gave his name.

'Who is there, Mary?' called out the lady of the house, who had heard the front door open and shut.

'Please'm,' replied the maid in a strangled voice, 'the Air Popham.'

In the course of a state visit to Australia by Elizabeth the Queen Mother and another member of the Royal Family, a garden party was held at which the two found themselves encompassed by an ever-narrowing circle of inquisitive Australians. The Queen Mother remained her smiling self throughout, but was heard to murmur, 'Please don't touch the exhibits.'

A short-sighted old lady who was ill in bed received a visit from, as she thought, the local vicar. After he had left, she told her young niece how much she appreciated the vicar's kindness in coming to call.

'But, Auntie,' said the niece, 'that wasn't the vicar, it was the doctor.'

'Was it?' replied her aunt. 'I thought the dear vicar was rather familiar.'

A young clergyman was 'in retreat' at a country house near Guildford and was not supposed to leave the house or its grounds without the permission of his superiors. Nevertheless he decided, one fine afternoon, to play truant and set out on foot for Guildford, but had the bad luck to encounter his bishop, who asked him what he was doing away from his place of retreat and whether he had obtained leave of absence.

'No, my Lord,' answered the young man, 'but I was moved by the Holy Spirit to go and do some shopping in Guildford.'

'Indeed,' replied the bishop, 'then all I can say is that either you or the Holy Spirit are in error. I live in Guildford and happen to know that today is early closing day.'

Talleyrand, when he was a minister of the French First Republic, was in the company of a colleague who was lamenting the difficulty of converting the French peasantry to Rationalism. What could one do to impress such people?

'Well,' rejoined Talleyrand drily, 'you might try getting crucified and rising again on the third day.'

Several men who had been involved in a serious road accident were brought to hospital on stretchers and the dead were separated from the living. One of those believed to be dead had been accompanied by his wife, who was mainly interested in the insurance money to which his death would entitle her.

As soon as she arrived, therefore, she approached one of the harassed doctors dealing with the emergency and, pointing to her husband on his stretcher, said:

'He's dead isn't he, doctor?'

'I'm afraid so, madam,' said the doctor, incautiously assuming that the judgment of the stretcher-bearers as to who was dead and who was not had been correct.

At this moment the woman's supposedly dead husband, who was in fact alive and had overheard the conversation, suddenly sat up on his stretcher and said:

'I'm not dead, doctor,'

'Lie down,' snapped his wife. 'The doctor knows.'

It is related that Miss Coco Chanel received a proposal of marriage from the English Duke of X. Her reply was that she felt unable to accept because in her view the world was already overstocked with Duchesses of X (the Duke having been several times married and divorced) whereas there was only one Coco Chanel.

A visitor to a country public house in the early part of the day observed an old man sitting on a bench outside with a vacant expression on his face. In the evening he paid another visit to the same public house and saw the old man still there. Having bought his pint of beer, he joined the old man on the bench and asked him whether he did not find life a trifle monotonous.

'Why, no sir,' replied the old man. 'I gets plenty of variety. Sometimes I sits and thinks and sometimes I just sits.'

Pierpoint Morgan was once approached by a friend who had often borrowed money from him in the past without repaying it.

'Will you lend me your ear,' began the friend.

'Certainly,' cut in Morgan, 'but nothing else.'

One of Bernard Shaw's plays called for a very large cast.

The first and second performances were not well attended and just before the beginning of the third performance a member of the cast, Mrs Patrick Campbell, looked through a peep-hole in the curtain to see whether the audience was any larger.

'How are we doing tonight?' enquired Shaw.

'Better than last night and the night before,' was the reply, 'but we are still in the majority.'

An old lady visiting London Zoo was disappointed to find that none of the lions or other large beasts of prey were visible, having apparently all retreated to the covered parts of their cages. She mentioned this to the keeper, who explained it was the mating season and that there was not much chance of the animals emerging for some little time.

'If I offered them a bun, do you think they would come out?' asked the old lady.

'Well, madam,' replied the keeper, 'would you?'

Two men were discussing a third.
'He thinks he is a wit,' said one of them.
'Yes,' replied the other, 'but he's only half right.'

In the middle of the American Civil War it was represented to President Lincoln by a deputation containing some of his more straitlaced supporters that General Grant, the successful Union general, should be relieved of his command on the ground of his intemperance. The President demurred on the ground that Grant was too valuable to lose.

'But,' said the leader of the deputation, 'he is a heavy drinker. Whiskey!'

'In that case,' replied Lincoln, 'find out what brand he drinks and send a case of it to each of his brother generals.'

Lady Astor, the first woman M.P., was delivering a speech and was interrupted by a heckler who shouted:

'Your husband's a millionaire, isn't he?'

'I hope so,' she replied, 'that's why I married him.'

Noel Coward was presenting one of his comedies in America at the same time as Lady Diana Cooper was acting the part of the Virgin Mary in a highly serious play entitled 'The Miracle.'

When in due course they met, Lady Diana observed:

'I saw your play, Noel, but I am afraid I did not laugh once.'

'Didn't you, darling?' replied Coward. 'I saw yours and simply roared.'

At the end of a hunt ball, a very clumsy dancer approached a former partner of his and said:

'May I have my last dance with you?'

'Well,' was the reply, 'as a matter of fact, you've already had it.'

Asked why he did not join a club Groucho Marx is reported to have replied:

'I wouldn't want to join any club that would accept me.'

Barrister (to witness): '*You say that the defendant was drunk.*'
Witness: '*Yes, sir, drunk as a judge.*'
Judge: '*You mean drunk as a lord?*'
Witness: '*Yes, my lord.*'

During the last war an English lady was entertaining some Polish officers in her house.

'I understand, captain,' she said to one of them, 'that you are married. Have you any children?'

'Alas, no madame,' replied the officer, 'my wife is unbearable.'

'I am afraid,' said another of the officers, 'that my friend's English is not yet quite perfect. He means that his wife is inconceivable.'

Upon this the third officer intervened with the words:

'I am sorry, but I fear that both my friends are wrong. What they mean is that the lady is impregnable.'

When Spencer Tracy first met Katherine Hepburn—they were to star in a film together—Miss Hepburn exclaimed:

'*I'm afraid I'm a little tall for you, Mr Tracy.*'

'*Never mind, Miss Hepburn.*' *replied Tracy,* '*I'll soon cut you down to my size.*'

Between the two world wars the Crown Prince of Japan sought entry to the aristocratic college of Christ Church, Oxford, but was rejected on the grounds that among his many titles was one which meant 'Son of God'. The Crown Prince then sought admission to another Oxford college—Magdalen—which was only by small margin, if at all, less aristocratic than the first choice. The head of Magdalen, who was a notorious and incorrigible snob, had no difficulty in accepting him. Referring to the Prince's title, 'Son of God', he said that the college already contained the sons of many 'distinguished gentlemen', and he could see no objection to increasing the number.

Young army officer, dealing with the case of a recruit charged with insulting behaviour:
'In what way did the accused insult you, Sergeant Major?'
'Sir, on entering the men's sleeping quarters at 9 a.m., I found the accused lying in bed at me.'

Oscar Wilde once wrote that he was unfortunately unable to accept an invitation he had received because of a subsequent engagement.

Lord Justice Darling, who lived in the early part of this century, was noted for the humorous remarks he made in court. He might, in fact, have been described as the comedian of the courts.

On one occasion, Darling was trying a case in which reference was made to the professional comedian Mr (later Sir) George Robey.

'Who,' enquired Darling, in real or affected ignorance, 'Is George Robey?'

'I understand, my lord,' replied Counsel, 'that he is the Darling of the music halls.'

John Wilkes, politician, journalist and rake of the eighteenth century, quarrelled violently with Lord Sandwich, who exclaimed:

'Sir, you will either die of the pox or on the gallows.'

To which Wilkes replied:

'Depending on whether I embrace your mistress or your principles.'

An oriental potentate had condemned a man to death, but had given his word that, in recognition of certain services which the man had rendered in the past, he might choose the manner of his death.

The man expressed his gratitude and said that, having thought the matter over, he would like to die of old age.

An attractive young woman in a very décolleté dress was wearing a necklace from which hung a tiny model aircraft. One of the young men present seemed unable to take his eyes off it, and the young lady remarked:

'I see you admire my little miniature.'

'Well,' replied the young man, blushing, 'actually, what I was admiring was its landing ground.'

An Anglican Christian was invited by a Jewish friend to attend a Jewish wedding in the local synagogue. He did so and was somewhat shocked by the seemingly frivolous and informal way in which the members of the Jewish congregation conducted themselves before the wedding service began. Nothing like this, he thought, could happen at a Church of England wedding. He confided his feelings to his Jewish friend, who replied:

' You must remember that we Jews have known the Lord much longer than you have.'

When Queen Victoria and the Prince Consort visited Eton, one of the pupils was asked how often he had been caned. In reply he quoted from the 6th Book of *The Aeneid*, the line *'Infandum, regina, jubes, renovare dolorem'* meaning 'Unspeakable, O Queen, is the pain you bid me renew.'

The reply was considered so apt that he was rewarded with a sovereign.

Before the introduction of Daylight Saving, a supporter of the scheme was trying to explain it to the curate of his parish.

'You see,' he said, 'you really get up at seven, but you pretend you're getting up at eight.'

'I see,' said the curate doubtfully, 'but isn't that rather deceitful?'

James Pride, the painter, made a point of dressing conventionally and eschewing the sloppy clothes favoured by most members of the artistic fraternity.

On one occasion, when Pride was wearing an unusually loud check suit, one of his fellow painters whose work was generally considered mediocre asked him:

'Why do you dress like a bookmaker when you are not a bookmaker?'

To which Pride replied:

'Why do you dress like an artist when you are not an artist?'

Young man to his dining partner:

'Can you tell me which of those gentlemen is Mr Robinson?'

'Why yes—the one with the grey moustache. I'm Mrs Robinson.'

'Yes, I know,' replied the young man. 'I thought you'd be sure to know.'

On hearing that the Bastille had been stormed by the mob, Louis XVI exclaimed to the Duc de la Rochefoucauld-Liancourt, a member of his court:

'C'est une révolte?'

'Non, Sire,' replied the duke, 'C'est une révolution.'

A Gentile was boasting of his noble ancestry to a Jewish friend.

'Why,' he said, 'an ancestor of mine was one of the barons who gave England Magna Carta.'

'Is that so?' replied the Jew. 'Well, one of my ancestors gave the world the Ten Commandments.'

During the First World War, when Egypt was a British Protectorate, Colonel T. E. Lawrence ('Lawrence of Arabia'), who was known to dislike social functions, had nevertheless been inveigled to a cocktail party in Cairo. Among those present was a lady of uncertain age who liked entertaining celebrities and wished to add Lawrence (to whom she had not been personally introduced) to her collection. Thinking to use the hot weather—the temperature was 92 degrees F—as an excuse for opening a conversation, she advanced upon Lawrence, vigorously plying her fan, with the words:

'92 to-day, Colonel Lawrence! Imagine it! 92 today!'

'Many happy returns, madam,' growled Lawrence.

Sir Robert Walpole served as Prime Minister under both George I and George II. Queen Caroline, the wife of George II, was anxious to enclose one of London's public parks for the exclusive use of the royal family, and sought the advice of Sir Robert. The latter, knowing how intensely unpopular such a proceeding would be, demurred on the ground that the cost would be too high. The Queen, however, was not to be put off and pressed him for an estimate. He replied:

'I fear, Madam, that it might cost as much as a couple of crowns.'

A woman was applying for a maintenance order against her husband, who was said to have deserted her for seven years and to have made no provision for her or his children.

'I understand,' said the magistrate, 'that you have three children, aged respectively, two, four and six. How exactly do you square this with your allegation that your husband has deserted you for seven years?'

'Well, your worship,' replied the woman, 'he keeps coming back to apologize.'

A barrister, asked for his opinion of a newly appointed High Court judge, replied:

'With a little more experience he'll be the worst judge in the Queen's Bench Division.'

The actress Zsa Zsa Gabor was asked by an interviewer how many husbands she had had. A little puzzled, she replied:
'You mean apart from my own?'

A man who was being pestered by a beggar said:
'I've nothing for you today. Come back tomorrow.'
'Well, all right,' said the beggar doubtfully, 'but I've lost a lot of money giving credit that way.'

In reply to a lady who said that she knew of only two painters in the world, Whistler and Velasquez, Whistler is reputed to have said:
'Why drag in Velasquez?'

Reply attributed to Napoleon on hearing of Nelson's first victory over the French Fleet:
'I cannot be everywhere.'

It is related of Bernard Shaw that he once opened his front door to find himself face to face with two earnest young men, one of whom had some pamphlets in his hand.
'Who are you and what do you want?' asked Shaw.
'We're Jehovah's Witnesses,' said one of them.
'Really?' replied Shaw, 'I'm Jehovah. How are we doing?'

In reply to lady who asked whether genius was hereditary, Whistler replied:

'I cannot tell you, Madam. Heaven has granted me no offspring.'

A well-known actress who had been living with a fellow member of the profession found him dining tête-à-tête with another woman. She advanced towards them smiling, but received from the man nothing but a frozen stare.

'What's the matter darling?' she asked sweetly. 'Don't you know me with my clothes on?'

Harold Nicholson and his wife were at a dinner-party and were asked by their hostess why, being both authors, they had never produced anything jointly.

'Oh, but we have,' replied Nicholson, 'we have two sons.'

Sir Malcolm Sargent, the conductor, was asked, at about the age of seventy, to what he attributed his advanced age.

'Well,' he replied, 'I suppose I must attribute it to the fact that I haven't died yet.'

Lady listening to the singing of a choir in a near-by church to ardent naturalist listening to the crickets:
'It's very beautiful, isn't it?'
'Yes. And the extraordinary thing is that they do it by rubbing their legs together.'

An Englishman in a French mountain village, where the air was exceptionally fresh and invigorating, took a seat in a café and remarked to the waitress who served him:
'Vous avez l'air très pur ici.'
'Oui, Monsieur,' replied the waitress, 'nous sommes très comme il faut.'

George Lansbury M.P., a much-loved member of the Labour Party, was never tired of portraying, almost with tears in his eyes, the hardships of the working class without putting forward any really practicable scheme for remedying them.
'What do you think of Lansbury?' asked one M.P. of another.
'Well,' was the reply, 'if only he wouldn't let his bleeding heart run away with his bloody head.'

A visitor to a small village accosted an elderly local and asked who was the oldest inhabitant.
'We 'aven't got one now, sir,' was the reply; 'we 'ad one, but 'e died three weeks ago.'

The question had arisen whether the Russian army could repel a foreign invasion, and the then Tzar of Russia, Nicolas I, said that his country had two generals on whom it could rely. Asked who they were he replied:

'General January and General February.'

That this was still true was discovered, to his cost, by Adolf Hitler on the occasion of his attack on Russia during the Second World War.

During the Peninsular War, the Duke of Wellington, on being asked what he thought of the latest reinforcements sent out from England, replied:

'I don't know what effect these troops will have on the enemy, but by God they frighten me.'

Indignant High Court Judge to a colleague:

'All these people sleeping together before they're married! I didn't sleep with my wife before we were married. Did you?'

'I don't know,' replied his colleague. 'What was her maiden name?'

Mahatma Ghandi, the Indian sage and reformer, was asked what he thought about Western civilisation.

'I think,' he said, 'that it would be very good idea.'